Firefighters

Laura K. Murray

seedlings

CREATIVE EDUCATION • CREATIVE PAPERBACKS

Published by Creative Education and Creative Paperbacks
P.O. Box 227, Mankato, Minnesota 56002
Creative Education and Creative Paperbacks
are imprints of The Creative Company
www.thecreativecompany.us

Design by Ellen Huber
Production by Grant Gould
Art direction by Rita Marshall
Printed in the United States of America

Photographs by Alamy (Aircraft crash and fire, Vastram),
Getty (Johner Images, Valerie Loiseleux, Maskot, Siwabud
Veerapaisarn/EyeEm), iStockphoto (kali9, nightman1965,
okanmetin), Shutterstock (Bellchalerm, Gorodenkoff, Kite_
stockfoto, LaKirr, potowizard, Prath, sraphotohut, Suchatbky,
thekovtun, urbans, Marianne Venegoni)

ISBN 9781640264106 (library binding)
ISBN 9781628329438 (paperback)
ISBN 9781640005747 (eBook)

LCCN 2020907010

TABLE OF CONTENTS

Hello, firefighters!

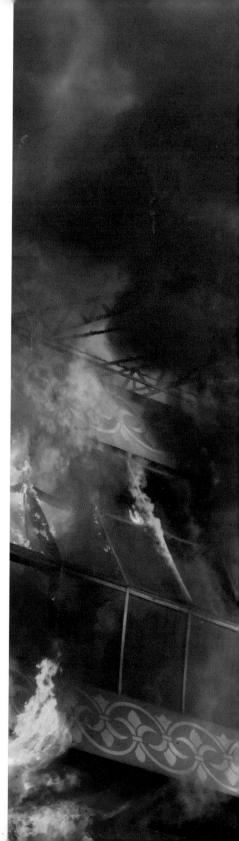

Firefighters help
in an emergency.
They go to
accidents.

They put out fires. They keep people safe.

Firefighters work in a fire station.

They sleep and eat there. They are ready to help.

Firefighters drive
fire trucks.

These have
ladders,
hoses, and
other tools.
They have
loud sirens.

Firefighters teach people how to be safe. They show how to keep forest fires from starting.

Special clothing helps keep them safe.

They wear a helmet and boots. A mask gives them air.

Firefighters
race to help.

They spray water or foam on a fire. They help people who are hurt.

Thank you, firefighters!

Picture a Firefighter

oxygen tank

mask

hose

boot

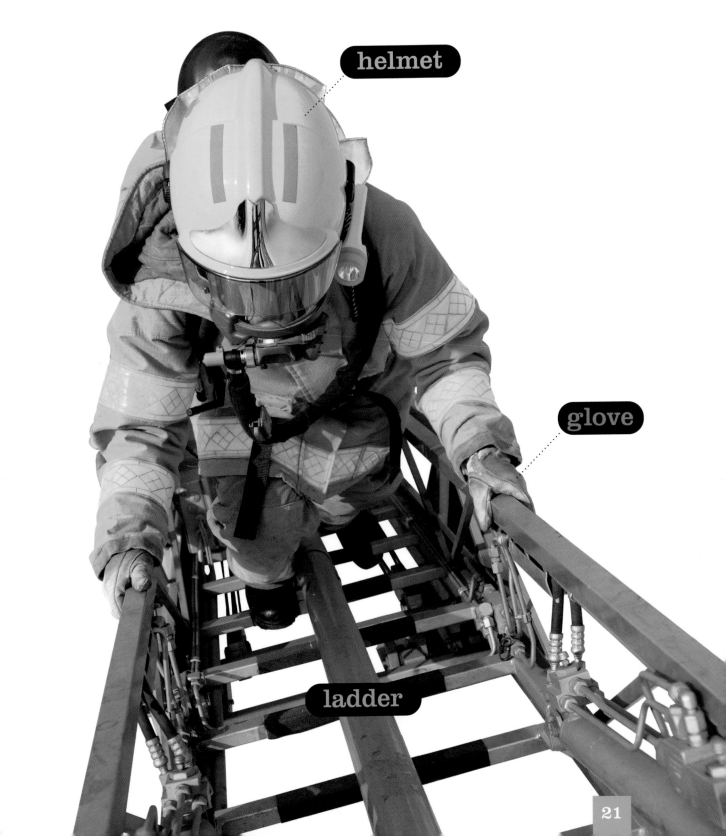

helmet

glove

ladder

Words to Know

fire station: where fire trucks and tools are kept

foam: a thick mixture made of small bubbles; helps put out fires

mask: a cover for the face

sirens: the parts of a vehicle that make loud, warning sounds

Read More

Bowman, Chris. *Firefighters*.
Minneapolis: Bellwether Media, 2018.

Keppeler, Jill. *Fire Trucks*.
New York: PowerKids Press, 2020.

Websites

Brigade Kids: Fire + Rescue
http://www.brigadekids.com.au

Sparky the Fire Dog
http://sparky.org

Index